解語者

The Keeper of Unspoken Words

解語者

The Keeper of Unspoken Words

Published by Oves Books 燕麥地書社

Designed by Vincent M. Hu

Manufactured in the United States of America
Oves Books are printed on acid-free paper
First published in the United States Cloth Bound in 2026

ISBN 979-8-9943499-1-5
Library of Congress Control Number: 2026900281

解語者
The Keeper of Unspoken Words

胡木貴 著

Poems by Vincent M. Hu

燕麥地書社 OVES BOOKS CINCINNATI OHIO

This poetry collection

is dedicated

to the three thousand and one nights of

Discourse, Attunement, and Ecstasy.

僅以此詩集

獻給

三千零一夜的

論道、解語和銷魂

目錄

Table of Contents

論道、解語、銷魂

Discourse、*Attunement*、*Ecstasy*

当一个词轻轻触碰，世界便在刹那间苏醒。

When a word touches, the world flickers awake.

解語者

黑與白的早晨，鋪滿魚鱗
五彩的身體醒來
鐵銹色橡樹葉，亂飛
你站立，天空下候鳥歸去

我欲止又言，那些
近乎耳語的黯淡
身體之初，青萍之末
被你傾聽的光輝照亮

我，在你的欲望中
夢見自己一匹狼，朝你靠近
利齒含著一枝棉花
彼此面龐，蘇醒的幻像

單行道，伸向冬日之海
燈塔對著藍色裂縫哼唱
把魚放回黑藍色潮汐
目送它遊動的脊背
含笑點頭，相聚或沉入
在彼此的自語裡閃爍

Keepers of the Unsaid

Black-and-white morning, scaled with fish.
A body of shifting colors wakes.
Rust-oak leaves, flying wild.
You stand—under a sky emptied of migrants.

I would speak, then not.
Those dimnesses, almost whisper.
The body's beginning, the reed's last edge—
all lit by the brightness of your listening.

I—inside your desire—
dream myself a wolf, moving toward you,
a cotton sprig between my sharp teeth.
Our faces: illusions stirring awake.

A one-way road, stretching to winter sea.
A lighthouse humming to a blue fracture.
Returning a fish to the black-blue tide,
watching the ripple of its traveling spine.
Smiling, nodding, meeting or sinking—
we flicker inside each other's quiet speech.

別驚惶

如果你看見
一匹馬
有大提琴的軀體
鐵錘的四蹄
長著雄雞的驕傲翅膀
鷓鴣的啼鳴
擺動藍色的魚尾
忽然間，他張開裂縫般的嘴，
化為一隻
戴著牢籠的豹
月光在牠眼中滴落
別驚惶，那是
我，在夢中
前來，和你聚會

Do Not Be Afraid

If you should see
a horse—
its body shaped like a cello,
four hooves forged like hammers,
bearing the proud wings of a rooster,
crying with a partridge's call,
its blue fish-tail swaying—
suddenly it opens a mouth like a fissure
and turns into
a leopard wearing a cage.
Moonlight drips from its eyes —
do not be afraid.
It is only me,
coming to meet you
from within a dream.

言詞之上

酒杯邊緣將散未散
的那縷嗡鳴，讓我們
懸浮，半醉半醒

我們，沒有
最小的量詞，忽略不計地
來捕獲它的巨大
也沒有
最虛化的詞，霧一般
來證明它的確鑿

無法用讚美
哄騙它唱
也不能用抹黑
來激怒它

無人知曉

沉沁在黑暗中
想要抓住那無法表達的東西
太迷人了

Above Words

The faint hum
gathering and dispersing
along the rim of the glass—
it lifts us, half-drunk, half-awake.

We have
no smallest measure, nothing
negligible enough
to capture its vastness;
nor do we have
the thinnest word, mist-like,
to prove its certainty.

No praise
can coax it into song.
No darkening
can provoke it.

No one knows.

Sinking into darkness,
wanting to grasp what cannot be said—
too alluring,

太悲傷了
太徒勞了
太短促了
太漫長了

好在我們可以
並肩目睹這一切

too sorrowful,
too futile,
too brief,
too long.

Still, we are able
to witness all of this
side by side.

私語

水沉入水裡
火回到火中
鳥在你髮間啼鳴
魚在我唇上遊動

Whisper

Water slips deeper into water.
Fire folds itself back into fire.
A bird sings in your hair
A fish glides across my lips.

耳朵的創世紀

一

萬物之嬰，應是
從耳朵誕生——
當側身傾聽，語詞穿越皮膚
山脈在聽小骨間隆起
河流於耳蝸的螺旋中潺潺
星辰在鼓膜震顫的夜幕裡閃爍

傾聽，是宇宙的煉金術
石頭因此獲得嘴唇
吐露音節，說出自身的輪廓
嘴唇開成一朵花
色彩如潮湧出，如夢賦形

耳朵是棱鏡，傾聽如觸手
在混沌中撫摸世界邊緣
於是，萬象蘇醒
在聲音的光中顯形

二

有了傾聽，就有了你我

Genesis of the Ear

I

The infant of all things
must have been born from the ear—
when we lean to listen, words pass through the skin,
mountains rise between the tiny bones,
rivers murmur through the spiral of the cochlea,
and stars flicker in the night-sky
trembling on the drum of the ear.

Listening is the alchemy of the universe.
Stones gain lips,
release syllables, speak their own contours.
Lips open like a flower,
color surging forth, dream taking form.

The ear is a prism; listening, a kind of touch—
feeling along the edges of the world in its chaos.
Thus the ten thousand things awaken,
taking shape in the light of sound.

II

With listening, you and I come into being.

我們以聆聽雕琢彼此的身影
將甘苦、笑淚融入耳畔的迴響
放入各自切膚的人生
你的呼吸輕拂我的耳廓
如潮汐拍膚，如星門洞開
你說「光」，我體內升起太陽
向日葵在眼底綻放金黃
我說「水」，你指縫淌出溪流
繞腕成湖，映出未說出的月亮

你說「火焰」，我獻出鯤鵬之羽
我言「深淵」，你拋下繩梯急切進來
夜裡你說「我在」
我的心跳應聲而起，時間滴答
我說「門」，你就推開
一同走入一個隱秘的房間
語言尚未命名的所在

三
傾聽，是一場蝴蝶的嬉戲
語詞自你唇間飛出, 栩栩然
意義搖曳不定，如光在水面折射
耳朵是港灣，收留遊蕩的音節

有時，蝴蝶迷霧中失向

We sculpt each other's outlines by hearing,
folding sweetness and bitterness, laughter and tears
into the echo beside the ear,
placing them into our separate, skin-deep lives.
Your breath brushes the rim of my ear—
like tides against the body, like a star-gate opening.
You say light, and a sun rises inside me;
sunflowers bloom gold behind my eyes.
I say water, and streams slip through your fingers,
circling your wrist into a lake
where an unspoken moon appears.

You say flame, and I offer the feather of a great bird.
I say abyss, and you put down a rope ladder, rushing in.
At night you say I'm here,
and my heartbeat answers, time ticking awake.
I say door, and you push it open—
we enter a hidden room together,
a place language has not yet named.

III

Listening is a butterfly's play.
Words lift from your lips, vivid, alive;
meaning wavers, like light refracted on water.
The ear is a harbor, sheltering wandering syllables.

Sometimes the butterfly loses its way in fog,

意義在晦暗中彷徨
傾聽，點燈照亮
蝴蝶偶會掀起颶風，語義折翅
遊離、推遲與變形：
我說「錨」，你卻漂向虛空
你低語「玫瑰」，我舌尖
嘗到一枚刺的甜血

共同世界，如此難以預設
我們用詞語試探彼此
用誤解靠近，用沉默確認
每一瞬傾聽，都濺出創世的火花
世界自反復的低語中成形

四

傾聽，是一座橋
連接你我生命的羊腸小道
我們攜手走過
道旁野花次第盛開
呦呦鹿鳴，歡歌嘉賓

傾聽，如焊接
縫合兩個世界的裂隙
拼接各自的視野
更大的星河在耳畔旋轉

meaning hesitates in the dimness.
Listening lights a lamp. Sometimes the butterfly
stirs a storm, meaning breaks its wings—
drifting, delayed, transformed.
I say anchor, and you drift toward emptiness.
You whisper rose, and on my tongue
I taste the sweet blood of a thorn.

A shared world is impossible to predict.
We probe each other with words, approach through
misunderstanding, confirm through silence.
Every instant of listening sparks a fire of creation;
the world forms itself from murmurs repeated.

IV

Listening is a bridge
linking the narrow paths of our lives.
We walk through it side by side,
wildflowers blooming along the way,
deer calling softly, welcoming guests.

Listening is a weld
sealing the fractures between two worlds,
joining our separate visions.
A larger galaxy turns beside the ear;

兩株孤柏的火焰交融
照亮更遼闊的夜空

我們在彼此的耳道裡
種下色彩、溫度、質地、時光——
相互傾聽，擁有一個共同身體
用同一唇瓣訴說
鑄就語詞的宇宙
在耳海的瞬間，永生

五
但世界，也被耳朵毀滅
如果充耳不聞
語詞如雪崩，化為噪音
唇齒間的星座，四散逃逸

你我共織的五彩錦緞裂解
歸於泥土、腐朽
你我共同世界的穹頂，裂開
坍塌，塵土漫天

世界淪為孤島，沉入晦暗
音樂將琴鍵
收回於寂靜的腹腔
寂靜，開始吞噬自身
連影子都不剩，無

the flames of two solitary cypresses merge,
illuminating a wider night.

In each other's ear-canals
we plant color, warmth, texture, time—
through mutual listening, we share a single body,
speak with the same petal of a mouth,
forge a universe of words,
and in the sea of the ear, become eternal.

V

But the world is also destroyed by the ear.
If we refuse to hear,
words avalanche into noise,
the constellations between our lips scatter.

The brocade we wove together unravels,
returns to soil, to rot.
The dome of our shared world cracks,
collapses, dust rising everywhere.

The world becomes an island, sinking into dimness.
Music withdraws its keys
into the abdomen of silence.
Silence begins to devour itself—
until not even a shadow remains.
Nothing.

致糾結的春風

一張黑白舊照片
黃昏的燈火
依然在對視的眼睛之間
微微上翹的嘴角
明亮的語詞，溫暖的撫掌
窗外大片鉛雲亂飛
壁上的弓影在杯中晃動

一匹古老特洛伊木馬
藏滿虛擬的愛人
夜闌人靜，潛入夢中
一次又一次攻陷
哦，冰雪聰明的春風
親愛的春風
你一直在和她們作戰嗎

To the Tangled Spring Wind

A black-and-white photograph.
The dusk-lit lamps
still burning between two gazes.
The faint lift of a mouth's corner,
bright words, a warm palm passing over.
Outside, sheets of leaden cloud scatter,
and the bow-shaped shadow on the wall
trembles inside the glass.

An ancient Trojan horse,
stuffed with virtual lovers
slips into dreams in the hush of night,
laying siege again and again.
Oh, spring wind—
clever as ice, clever as snow—
dear spring wind,
have you been fighting them
all this time?

四月還會下雪

夜複一夜，夢見
空轉的木馬願意說話了
甚至，指尖觸到溫暖
一枝棉花的純白火焰

再一次驚醒，黎明
牙齒彈奏大提琴的弦
風聲大作
像一群麻雀同時飛離

地上亮，天上暗
原來，四月還會下雪
一片片，阿司匹林
遠方汽笛又響起

April Still Snows

Night after night, I dream
the idle wooden horse
finally willing to speak—
even the fingertips touch warmth,
a cotton blossom's pure white flame.

Again I startle awake. Dawn.
Teeth pluck the strings
of an unseen cello.
The wind rises—
like a flock of sparrows
lifting all at once.

The ground bright, the sky dim.
So this is how April still snows:
flake after flake, aspirin falling.
And from far off,
a siren sounds again.

出差在外

能做什麼，在四月
一個人來到威斯康辛
無非在麥迪森城最好的餐館
擠在一群穿著動人臉孔的陌生人中
露出過分的笑容
喝酒，喉結不斷播報廣告
誇耀公司最棒的產品

嘎然而止的談笑風生
清晰的疼痛，月亮一樣升起來
滿湖的水如浩大锤击
鍛打刀坯，刃光刀影浩大

春寒沒有回心轉意
如同一部老電影重播倒帶
所有的花退回成尖銳小釘子
在牆上釘住春天的幻象

親愛的春風在遠方吹
親愛的春風在遠方吹

Traveling for Work

What is there to do, in April,
arriving alone in Wisconsin—
nothing but sit in Madison's finest restaurant,
pressed among strangers wearing
their most persuasive faces,
offering an exaggerated smile,
drinking, the Adam's apple broadcasting ads,
praising the company's finest product.

The chatter stops abruptly.
A clean pain rises, like a moon lifting.
The lake water strikes like a massive hammer,
forging a blade blank, its glint and shadow immense.

The spring chill refuses to turn back—
like an old film rewound and replayed.
Every flower retreats into a sharp little nail,
pinning the illusion of spring to the wall.

Dear spring wind blowing far away,
dear spring wind blowing far away.

冬天的海

你還在遠方嗎
那家臨海的小旅館
透過鹽反復咬蝕的窗櫺
凝視那無形的地平線？

對，你提起過冬天的海
那些凍住的浪濤，一個人的沙灘
冬眠的魚群
遊弋在往日的碎片裡

風不時到來，打聽
一隻沉船的下次啟航日期
叩擊四處裂縫的艙門
鏽錨低語著遺忘的航線
而雪一直飄著
如同海上的藍火焰

嗯，你已無法寫長長的信
故鄉，每日有許多村莊消失
古老街巷，潮水退去
留下，查無此人的郵戳

The Winter Sea

Are you still far away—
in that little seaside inn, gazing through
the window frame gnawed by salt,
toward the horizon that refuses to appear?

Yes, you once spoke of the winter sea—
those frozen waves, a beach meant for one,
the fish gone into hibernation,
wandering through fragments of the past.

Wind comes now and then, inquiring
about the next departure of a sunken ship,
knocking on the cabin doors full of cracks,
the rusted anchor whispering its forgotten routes.
And the snow keeps falling,
like blue flames over the sea.

You can no longer write long letters.
In the homeland, villages vanish day by day.
Old streets, the tide pulls back—
leaving behind postmarks
that say: no such person found.

遠方的港口

我身體的深處
沉睡著一個初醒的你
遠涉重洋的另一個你
收起睫毛上的帆影
前來認領她的今生

而你的血脈的航道裡
那還在夢中騎木馬的我
勒住轠繩，質問
滿面風塵的這個我：
外鄉人，為何來遲

這樣遠方的海，不息
隨時聚散的港口
一種逃難和節慶的氣氛
英語與漢語，混合著
故鄉樟樹與鐵錨的氣息

四人在一起，亦悲亦喜
打量著對方身體裡的自己——
稀薄的翅，磨損的蹄

The Distant Port

Deep in my body
sleeps a just-awakened you;
another you, crossing oceans,
folds away the sails trembling on her lashes,
arriving to claim this life of hers.

And in the channels of your blood
the me still riding a wooden horse in dreams
pulls the reins tight, demanding
of this dust-covered me:
Stranger—why are you late.

Such a far-off sea, never still;
a port that gathers and scatters at any moment,
carrying the scent of flight and festival,
English and Chinese mingling
with camphor from home
and the iron breath of anchors.

The four of us together—joy and sorrow both—
studying the selves lodged inside each other's bodies:
thin wings, worn hooves,

四面相互映照的鏡子：
正要啟程的唇，剛抵達的眼

four mirrors reflecting one another—
lips about to depart, eyes just arriving.

月光蓍草

路遇一種從未見過的花
得知名叫“月光蓍草”
八月風中，搖曳著慷慨的黃金
花瓣，熟悉的眼神
來自一個從未抵達的記憶
我彎腰，呀了一聲
它幾乎在我一生中缺席

就像你，早晨和黃昏
在不同角度的光線裡微笑著
洗好的菜，在漏斗裡均勻呼吸
拿著家信，怔怔地出神
為人世瑣事輕皺眉頭
可至今，那場景我尚未得見

Moonlight Yarrow

I came upon a flower never seen before,
and learned its name, moonlight yarrow.
In the August wind, it swayed with a generous gold—
petals holding a gaze I somehow recognized,
from a memory that never managed to arrive.
I bent down, gasped softly.
It had been missing from almost my entire life.

Just like you—morning and dusk,
smiling in different angles of light;
the washed vegetables breathing evenly in the colander;
holding a letter from home, you gaze distance;
the slight furrow of your brow
over the small troubles of the world.
And yet, even now, I have never seen that scene.

羽毛

粗大韁繩系著一片羽毛
但無法系住，它太輕了
充滿欲求，輕得不能再輕

羽毛飄起來了
對秋陽，它亮出燦爛的剖面
誰在得意地輕笑

秋風漩渦中，遲疑又堅定
它應該來自一隻雄鳥
寂寞自足，天生不羈

羽毛飄升起時
有一雙眼睛
正被它的顫動牽掛
濕潤的黑玉，閃耀

Feather

A thick rope ties down a single feather—
but cannot hold it, for it is too light,
filled with wanting, light beyond light.

The feather lifts.
To the autumn sun, it unfolds brilliant cross-section.
Someone, somewhere, lets out soft laugh.

Hesitant yet resolute in the whirl of autumn—
it must have come from a male bird,
self-sufficient in its solitude, born untamed.

As the feather rises,
a pair of eyes
is caught by its trembling—
wet black jade, shining.

歸來

迷失的腳步
徑直走回了家門

那是一種溫柔的顫慄
撥亮了
歸人的面容

從你眼中飲水
就像夜，從白中汲取黑
滿溢我未醒的河床

用你的唇
呼喚著我自己

Return

Lost footsteps
walk straight back to the door.

A gentle trembling—
it lights up
the face of the one returning.

To drink water from your eyes
is like night drawing black from the white,
filling my riverbed not yet woken.

With your lips
I whisper my name

地址不明，語言未竟

不同的坐标，活着同一个巨大瞬间

Address unknown, the language unfinished.

At different coordinates, we live the same vast instant.

親愛的生活

皺巴巴的光鮮生活
千人千面的世界到處都一樣
變為異國的故鄉
寄居而成故里的別處
在生疏母語的不精煉表達中相遇

三千零一夜的纖維
風吹棉葉，棉花照月
蜂巢珍藏的苦蜜
牙齒發燙蛀洞的涼氣
流進彼此內心裂開之處

日夜愛著，就是沒做愛
就像許多人坐一起
吃晚餐，或隔夜剩飯
低頭滑各自手機、傻笑
不撫摸就同床共枕

又一場秋雨落下
擊打一座廢棄的車站屋頂
親愛的生活，地址
不明，語言未竟

Dear Life

Wrinkled, glossy life—
a world with thousand faces,
yet everywhere the same.
A homeland in a foreign land, and elsewhere
now is home after a long stay. We meet
in expressions with rusty mother tongue.

The fibers of three thousand and one nights—
wind stirring cotton leaves under the moon;
the bitter honey stored in the hive;
chill air seeping from a burning tooth hollow—
into the cracks inside us.

Love without making love—
like so many people sitting together
have over dinner, or leftovers,
heads bowed, scrolling their phones, smirking
sharing a bed without touching.

Another autumn rain falls,
striking the roof of an abandoned station.
Dear life—your address unknown,
your language unfinished.

亂髮

那浴後的亂髮
火焰般燃燒
它引領了秋天的時尚

這些雨絲，也這般
斜斜地，燃燒我的窗戶

Tangled Hair

That tangle of hair after the bath
burns like flame—
it sets the fashion for autumn.

And strands of rain,
slanting the same way,
are burning my window.

在人間

北風溫暖地刮著
你我的童話中，呈現的
還有其它的事物
旅途上，丟失錢包和手機
沒記住任何人的電話號碼
太平間，你與逝世父親
最後的沉默對坐

晝夜顛倒的時差，通紅的眼睛
矗立陌生的故鄉街頭
不知該乘幾路車，往哪個方向回家
一隻鞋子也在夢裡走失

一位男主播去世了
年輕時曾聽過他主持的“動物世界”
一群烏鴉，正人君子聚在那兒
在逝者的名字上築巢，呱噪著
在混亂的羽毛間翻找其曾經的失德

美好生活就這麼不完美持續
十年像同一天醒來

Among the Living

The warm north wind blows.
In the fairy tale of you and me,
other things appear as well—
losing a wallet and a phone on the road,
not remembering anyone's phone number;
in the morgue, you and your dead father
sitting in your final silent face-to-face.

Jet lag turning day and night upside down,
eyes red, standing on hometown's a strange street
not knowing which bus to take for home.
Even a shoe goes missing in a dream.

A male TV host has died.
When young, I watched his show Animal World.
A flock of crows—upright gentlemen— caws there,
building nests on the dead man's name,
rummaging through the tangled feathers
for his former misdeeds.

A good life continues in imperfection—
ten years waking as if to the same day.

第一千零一枚月亮從棉絮中升起
感歎著，如在同一座城多好

大口地吸氧，像那位
年過的半百茱蒂在街口
灰白頭髮風中飄浮，一絲不亂
等候，心怦怦跳如撞鹿

就像一同出生，奔入
萬家燈火中的旅館
留下天堂的淩亂
秋天去大都會博物館
烏鴉在畫框裡啄食童年的聲音

其實，比身邊的近還近
所有生活變故，都不離左右
彼此尚未寫出的文字
早已被相互讀過
尚未親觸的手，一直十指緊扣

The 1001 moon rises from the cotton,
marveling—what if wake up in the same city.

Deep breaths of oxygen,
like Judy standing at the street corner
her gray-white hair floating in the wind,
not a strand out of place, waiting, her heart thudding
like a startled deer.

As if we were born together, rushing
into a hotel lit by ten thousand households,
leaving behind heaven's mess.
In autumn, at the Met, crows peck at the sound
of childhood inside the picture frames.

In truth, closer than close—
every shift in life never far from our sides.
The words we have not yet written
already read by one another;
the hands not yet touched
already interlaced, finger by finger.

遠方花開

幾乎沒有七座山七條河
一隻獅子在紙上做夢
一朵花在遠方開放
人們都說如沐春風

晾衣繩掛著年輕的舊襯衣
孤獨的水龍頭在草地漏水
五月落日像只紅狐狸
野鴿子一直咕咕啼鳴

見過風見過雨見過下刀子
聽過冥王星的歌聲
野花紛紛喊你的名字
可我從來沒有見過你

你的微笑是我看不見的那朵花
你的歎息是我握不著的那芳香
遠方花開，遠方花開
遠方花開，遠方花開

A Flower in the Distance

Almost no seven mountains and rivers—
a lion is dreaming on paper, a flower
blooms far away, and people who see it
say it feels like bathing in spring sunlight.

An old shirt from youth on the clothesline
a lonely faucet leaks onto the grass;
the May sunset is a red fox,
and wild pigeons keep cooing and cooing.

I have seen wind, seen rain,
seen knives falling from the sky;
I have heard the singing of Pluto.
Wildflowers call your name
one after another—yet I have never seen you.

Your smile is the flower I cannot see;
your sigh is the fragrance I cannot hold.
A flower blooms in the distance—
a flower blooms in the distance.

山河安靜

節日彩燈的笑聲裡
鄰居孩子們手捧星星跑開

一位盲歌手在唱聖母瑪利亞
燭光在臉上晃動

燭光上，我向你走來
一片雪，赤足
穿過你不在的街道

冬日的山河安靜

Quiet Mountains and Rivers

In the laughter of holiday lights,
holding stars in hands, kids run off.

A blind singer is singing to the Virgin Mary;
candlelight wavers across his face.

On that candlelight,
I walk toward you—
a flake of snow, barefoot,
crossing the street
where you are not.

the mountains and rivers of winter
are quiet.

收垃圾日

空了的垃圾桶
嗵嗵地，扔回車道
收集垃圾的工人
在每戶門前重複同樣的動作
此起彼伏的垃圾桶
傾訴生活的快樂與無奈
或沉默不語，獨自活著
空洞的回聲
拓寬了冬天的晨霧

現在，八點鐘的陽光
透過高高安靜的空樹枝
星辰在目力之外閃耀
人們紛紛在路上
你也趕往公司
一直沒想到這個問題
憧憬了這麼多年
倘若，真在一起過
會有什麼樣的生活垃圾

Garbage Day

The emptied trash bins
thud back onto the driveway.
The workers collecting garbage
repeat the same motion at every door.
Bin after bin, rising and falling,
confess the joys and helplessness of daily life—
or say nothing, living alone.
Their hollow echoes
widen the winter morning fog.

Now, the eight-o'clock sunlight
filters through tall, quiet, bare branches.
Stars shine just beyond sight.
People are already on the road;
you too hurry toward the office.
I never thought about this question—
after longing for so many years:
If we really lived together,
what kind of household trash
would we make?

鋒利的菊花

菊花，终于开出
参差不齐的狼牙
透出，淡粉色的锋利
插在水晶瓶中

脱离土壤的花枝
以暮色的寂静为养
以瓶壁棱形
切割自己的幻影

还能有更锋利的花瓣
还能咬得更深？
欢喜，从古老的悲伤里升起
加速的黄昏，颤抖
慢了下来，几乎静止
惟薄刃在呼吸

Sharp Chrysanthemums

Chrysanthemums have finally bloomed—
uneven wolf-teeth,
revealing a pale-pink sharpness,
I set them in a crystal vase.

Cut from the soil,
the stems feed on the stillness of dusk,
and with the vase's faceted walls
slice through their own illusions.

Can petals grow sharper still?
Can they bite deeper?
Joy rises from ancient sorrow.
The accelerating dusk trembles,
slows, nearly stops—
only the thin blade keeps breathing.

傳染性夢魘

終於回到故國，在夢中
青磚黛瓦上，塔形的紅瓦松
在長江的微風中搖曳
突然恐慌，因為再也不能
返回僑居多年的他鄉
俄亥俄河畔，我親植的繡球花
在後院盤根錯節

腦海閃過一絲亮
身體卻被封印在雙面鏡中
出去是進來，背影長著眼睛
我拼盡全力，喊出聲
玻璃猛然碎裂
半睡半醒的喘息
半在他國，半在故鄉

讀一會書兒吧，黎明
尚未降臨關山重重的世界

我把夢告訴了你
儘量輕描淡寫
像倒空一瓶隔夜的水

Contagious Nightmare

At last, I return to my homeland—
in a dream. On blue-grey bricks and dark tiles,
tower-shaped red-tile pines
sway in the Yangtze breeze.
Suddenly, panic—for I can no longer
go back to the foreign land where I lived for years:
Along Ohio River, the hydrangeas I planted
are spreading their roots through the backyard.

A flash of light crosses my mind,
yet my body is sealed inside a double-sided mirror.
Going out is coming in, eyes on my back.
I shout with all my strength—
the glass shatters.
Half-asleep, half-awake, my breath stumbles,
half in one country, half in the other.

Read a little, as dawn has not yet reached
this world of layered mountain passes.

I told you the dream,
as lightly as I could,
like emptying a bottle of overnight water.

結果在你心裡縈回了好久
像吃進頑石消化不開

兩個世界的邊緣
硬峭又模糊
那兩扇門，別處或此地
一直敞開著又一直緊鎖著
我們碰啊撞啊

But it long lingered in your heart
like swallowing a stubborn stone

The edges of two worlds—
hard and blurred.
Those two doors, elsewhere or here,
always wide open and locked.
We keep colliding, again and again.

棉花和鐵

隔著七座山七條河
一片 棉花和一塊鐵躍躍欲試
準備攜手同遊

無論如何使勁按著他們的衝動
但無法按住
就像無法阻止春枝發芽

它們一起飄飛起來了
棉花白，鐵漆黑
以未說出的異類詞語作燃料

一位女孩在念辛波斯卡
在一個失約的火車站
看著旁人在相聚

棉花和鐵，浮在那一瞬
聽著女孩感歎：
他們接吻
並不以我們的嘴唇

棉花和鐵，滯了滯

Cotton and Iron

Across seven mountains and rivers,
a piece of cotton and a block of iron
grow restless, ready to travel together.

No matter how hard pressing down their impulse,
you cannot hold it—just as you cannot stop
spring branches from budding.

They rise together,
cotton white, iron pitch-black,
fueled by unsaid, mismatched words.

A girl is reciting Szymborska
in a train station where someone failed to arrive,
watching others reunite.

Cotton and iron, suspended
in that instant, hear the girl sigh:
They kiss—
but not with our lips.

Cotton and iron falter, just a little.

幾乎，不堪其輕而墜落
又難負其重而飄去

在場的鏽跡
還原成缺席的纖維

遠方的火車終於來了
但沒有人上車

Almost, unable to bear the lightness, they fall;
unable to bear the weight, they drift away.

The rust present in the scene
reverts to the fibers of absence.

The distant train finally comes—
but no one boards.

沙啞的歌手

低語縫隙裡的微熙晨光
讓我們心生憐憫

就像聽見，冬日的風
在紐約街頭遊蕩
為自己尋找一道溫暖裂縫

穿藍色雨衣的老男人
曾經的灰袍僧罩著烈焰
歌聲沙粒般一路撒下

有誰能量出
一千個吻的深

他且行且歌，走近走遠
誰能如何領養
他的那位哥們兼情敵

The Hoarse Singer

The morning rays in seams of whispers
makes pity rising in us.

As if hearing winter wind
wandering the streets of New York,
searching for a warm crack to slip into.

The old man in a blue raincoat—
once a gray-robed monk wrapped in flame—
scatters his voice like grains of sand.

Who could measure
the depth of a thousand kisses.

He walks and sings, near and far.
And who could ever adopt
his buddy—a rival of love.

共同醒來

隔著不曾遊歷的河、山
共同醒來

風吹奏各自的屋頂瓦片
吹奏心中竅孔
那些深藏的無聲音符

冬林搖晃，一場溫暖的雪
正在我們身內
睜開，嬰兒的眼睛
相互辨認

Waking Together

Across rivers and mountains
we have never traveled,
we wake together.

The wind plays the tiles
on each of our roofs,
plays the hidden apertures
of the heart—those silent notes
buried deep.

The winter forest sways;
a warm snow
is opening inside us,
like an infant's eyes
waking,
recognizing one another.

清晨應無限可延

幾乎每次，話語剛入港
清晨總是忍無可忍地結束
系住錨鏈的星星也退隱
馬達在路上轟鳴，透亮朝陽下
謀生的人影匆匆亂晃

那一分鐘漆黑的生命啊

上午，中午，乾脆一整天
為何不都折疊
放入清晨的定義
或者，將喋喋不休的低語者
合二為一成大露珠

在荷葉上，任其肆意滾動
交換澄明的黑暗
以遺憾，焊接時光的缺口
饑渴時，相濡以語詞
或一起人間蒸發

Let Morning Infinitely Extended

Almost every time words just reach the harbor,
morning loses its patience and ends,
and stars tied to the anchor chain slip away.
Engines roar on the road under the fresh sun,
the shadows of those making a living
stagger, blur.

Alas, that minute of pitch-black life.

Why not fold morning, noon,
even the entire day
into the definition of dawn—
or merge the ceaseless whisperers
into one great dewdrop

rolling on a lotus leaf,
trading lucid darkness
for the chance to weld
time's fractures with regret;
and when hunger comes,
moisten each other with words—
or evaporate together from the world.

數到三就動身

北風已吹過一千座山
吹過所有的窗戶
太陽已照耀匆匆上班的車流
廢氣在寒冷中閃亮

而室內，兩雙眼睛
捨不得睜開
永遠數不完一二三

時鐘滴答，傾聽
他們用更精確的小數點
延長溫暖，延長笑容的弧度
用零點一秒延長永恆
就在這二點九九和三之間
傷損的事物又完好如初
逝去的青春重新開始

Set Out on the Count of Three

The north wind has already blown
across a thousand mountains,
past every window.
The sun is shining in the rush-hour traffic;
exhaust gleams in the cold.

But indoors, two pairs of eyes
unwilling to open
can never finish
counting one, two, three.

The clock ticks, listening
as they use ever finer
decimal points to extend warmth,
to lengthen the curve of a smile—
to stretch eternity
by a tenth of a second.
In that space between 2.99 and 3,
what was damaged
is whole again,
and youth begins anew.

凍雨，推遲兩小時

鬍子拉碴的水中月
蓬頭素面的鏡中花

隔著冬日荒涼的山河
熱切說宇宙人生
雞毛蒜皮，路上薄冰

溫暖的手掌
相互握著空氣

幾個傳染的哈欠
咧開嘴，兩人無比幸福地
嘎嘎直笑

各自的窗外
冰雨絲，縫合著深淵
我們，聽著一針一線
穿梭於寂靜

你突然問：
這場縫合，何時
能抵達我們的岸邊？

Icy Rain, Delayed Two Hours

The unshaven moon in the water,
the unkempt flower in the mirror.

With the winter mountains and rivers
in the between, we speak with fervor
of the universe, of life—
trivialities, thin ice on the road.

Warm palms
holding only air.

A few contagious yawns,
mouths opening wide, the two of us laughing
helplessly, happily.

Outside each of our windows,
threads of freezing rain stitch the abyss shut.
We listen to each stitch
passing through silence.

Then you ask, suddenly:
When will this stitching
reach our shore.

章魚

一隻八爪魚
將她從沙漠裡打撈起來
她還深溺在虛空
滾燙的冰雪，驚鴻般撲騰
黃昏的飛蛾正四處落下
哦，好漢，救命

她需要更多的窒息
來獲取足夠氧氣
需要以更緊的纏繞、囚縛
博得更大自由、飛躍
這些巨大細緻入微的觸角
外星人的吸盤，可抽空一切

柔鋼繞指般開啟
對，一瓣瓣，解開
像春天雨滴的手指
打開第一朵玫瑰
開啟生死，萬劫不復
每一次 吐氣如蘭

這途中的每一道風景

Octopus

An octopus
hauls her up from the desert.
She is still drowning in the void—
scalding ice, fluttering like a startled bird;
moths of dusk fall everywhere.
Oh my hero, help.

She needs more suffocation
to draw enough oxygen,
needs tighter coils, tighter captivity
to win greater freedom, greater flight.
These vast, meticulous arms,
alien suckers capable of emptying anything.

Soft steel unfurls around her fingers—
yes, petal by petal, it opens,
like spring rain-fingers
opening the first rose,
opening life and death, no return
from any of it.
Each exhale orchid-soft.

Every landscape along the way,

任何細節，大可探幽取勝
世上可有任何事物
比水面空空的渡船更憂傷

噓，別錯過，那些
進入靈魂的秘道
以如此牢牢吸住
她搭救了她的拯救者
讓章魚真正擁有了八爪

every detail, invites its own descent.
Is there anything in this world
more sorrowful
than an empty ferry on still water?

Hush—don't miss
those secret passages
entering the soul.
By holding so tightly,
she rescues her rescuer,
and the octopus finally possesses
all eight arms.

深信彼此的切膚存在

便是愛，便是真理

Believing in each other's profound being—
that is love, that is truth.

一分鐘

你說，還可以再給你
一分鐘，那是
六十次宇宙的心跳

但是
一分鐘水火可以交溶嗎
一分鐘可以越過七座山七條河嗎
一分鐘岩石可以漂浮如風的書頁嗎
一分鐘可以想像一座不存在的城市嗎

一分鐘可以穿越鏡面迷宮找到彼此的影子嗎
一分鐘可以喂飽餓馬嚼碎草原的歌謠嗎
一分鐘可以聽完環形廢墟的無限敘事嗎
一分鐘可以讓裂隙酒醒吐出真言嗎

一分鐘可以數完天上的星星嗎
一分鐘可以扶起夜雨後的牡丹嗎
一分鐘可以聽懂一個沉默嗎
一分鐘可以完成創世紀嗎

一分鐘可以是一生嗎

One Minute

You say you can give me
one more minute—that is
sixty heartbeats of the universe.

But— in a minute
can water and fire merge?
can seven mountains and rivers be crossed?
can stone float like a page of wind-blown paper?
can one imagine a city that does not exist?

In a minute
can we cross a mirrored maze
and find each other's shadows?
can we feed a starving horse
the songs it chews from the grassland?
can we finish listening to the tale of a round ruin?
can we let the fissure sober up and speak its truth?

Can we count all the stars in the sky?
Can we lift a peony after night rain?
Can we understand a silence?
Can we complete a genesis?

Can a minute be a lifetime?

低語者

蝸蟻細小身體裡
滋養著沒有疆界的心臟

靠在一粒巨大玉米
交換細小、禁忌的詞

所有生活裂縫鍍上金邊
所有永恆事物都整裝離去

他們，從真實的裂縫中取出夢境
從永恆中取出短暫的欣喜

有好一陣，他們不說話
讓落霞與孤鶩在耳邊略過

星星墜落虛空，沙啞的嗓聲
透過手機螢幕、城市噪音

指定兩位低語者
繼承最後天真的暗影

The Whisperers

Inside the ant's tiny body
a borderless heart is being nourished.

Leaning against a giant kernel of corn,
they trade small, forbidden words.

Every crack in life is gilded;
and eternal thing packed is slipping.

They lift dreams out of the fissures of the real,
lift brief delight out of eternity.

For a long while they say nothing,
letting sunset and lone wild-duck
brush past their ears.

Stars fall into the void;
a hoarse voice passes through
phone screens and city noise.

Two whisperers are appointed
to inherit the last
innocent shadow.

黃昏點燈

一年將盡，鳥都已飛走
松針也落滿一地
蕭瑟連著蕭瑟，空氣凜冽
但語句卻冒著熱氣，
極易覺溫暖
靠近，哪怕再細微

樹在曠野疾行，寒風撥弦
帶來少時熟悉的氣息
走向遠方時，路旁
說不定有塊岩石會打開門
邀請說，*進來暖和一下吧*

天色向晚，欲雪未雪
壁爐中，松柴劈啪燃燒
好看的身影在牆上晃動
小獸醒來，豎起善聽的耳
用你的眼神，向我眨眼
好吧，我也同意
秋冬之交是一個美妙時候
让我们黄昏点灯

Lighting a Lamp at Dusk

The year ending, the birds leaving.
Pine needles cover the ground.
Bleakness spreading, the air sharp—
yet words give off steaming,
it is easy to feel their warmth
getting close, even a little.

Trees hurry across vast fields,
wind singing on the strings
brings back a childhood scent.
Walking toward the distance,
you might find a rock by the roadside
opening a door, inviting you in:
come warm yourself.

Evening deepens, snow almost.
Pine logs crackle in the fireplace,
a beautiful shadow moves on the wall.
A small creature wakes, ears lifted to listen.
It blinks at me with your eyes.
All right—I agree:
The turn of autumn into winter is marvelous.
Let us light up at dusk.

破曉

月亮還在找尋
遺忘在秋葉間的頭顱
但天亮了

溫暖的薄霜上
腳印正聆聽著汽笛
辨認方向

害羞的熊
長出鳥的羽毛
飛走了

那不曾抵達的地方
飽滿的漿果
在十月林中的深處

在世界兩個不同角落，我們
切膚地棲居在同一瞬間

深信彼此的切膚存在
便是愛，便是真理

Down

The moon is still searching
for the head it lost among autumn leaves—
but morning has arrived.

On warm, thin frost,
footprints listen to the whistle of a train,
trying to tell which way to go.

A shy bear
grows the feathers of a bird
and flies away.

That place we never reached—
its ripe berries
lie deep in the October woods.

In two different corners
of the world, we live keenly,
in the same instant.

To believe in each other's
profound existence—
that is love,
that is truth.

我美我先睡

落日除去衣衫
山河血紅，哀傷胴體裸露
冬天，金色獵戶星座
總是在黃昏時升起
對著虛空，彎弓搭箭

此刻，窗外北風呼嘯
風向標嘎吱作響，指向遠方
不起眼的一天，又將過去
錦衣上，補丁重疊
生活的針腳，淩亂綿密

熄燈前，有什麼
可以安之若素，含笑去睡
蕭瑟的世界，溫暖的你
兩個世界分別沉入黑甜

It's Beautiful to Sleep First

The sunset sheds its clothes,
blood-red landscape, desolate bodies laid bare.
In winter, the golden Orion
always rises at dusk,
bow drawn, aiming into the void.

Right now, north wind howls outside,
the vane creaks, pointing toward the distance.
Another unremarkable day is slipping.
On brocade garments, patches overlap—
the stitches of life, messy and dense.

Before lights go out, what is there
that lets one rest easy,
go to sleep with a smile.
A barren world, a warm you—
two worlds sinking separately
into sweet blackness.

我帥我先醒

冬晨，一個人，醒成
一隻蝴蝶，跌出夢境
栩栩然，華麗的斷翅
落於一個被收走梯子的沙漠

剛剛蒸發的綠洲地圖

這似是那夢境的廢墟
你的氣息蜿蜒
將一痕月影彎成魚鉤
打撈笑聲的殘骸

倒淌河，黃沙半掩
散架的鐘錶喘息
草蛇灰線，伏延千里
螢幕上，蝴蝶的爪印
在你的已讀和未讀之間
走走停停

窗外，風大作
一切蹤影，正被吹回
那扇虛掩的入睡之門

It's Handsome to Wake First

Winter morning, a person wakes
as a butterfly, falling out of a dream—
vivid, a splendid broken wing
dropping into a desert
where the ladder has been taken away.

The map of an oasis just evaporated.

This seems to be the ruin of that dream.
Your breath winds through it,
bending a trace of moonlight into a fishhook
to haul up the wreckage of laughter.

Reverse-Flowing River, half-buried in yellow sand,
a dismantled clock pants for air.
Like a trail of subtle clues, the truth
only emerges at the end.
On the screen, the butterfly's claw-prints
wander and pause
between your read and unread.

Outside, the wind rises.
Every trace is being blown back
toward that half-open door of sleep.

铁的收获季

冬日是收穫鐵的季節
疾風中，各種鐵的聲音
混入碎冰，不絕於耳

悲傷撒落的鐵屑
錘擊孤獨時，那崩掉的缺片
舊傷的鐵銹
掉在地上，發芽，生長
有的結出更大的鐵錘
有的，竟生出羽毛
有的，長出暈血的刀鋒
有的開成利針，柔軟地
堵塞天空的漏洞

其實，你也可以
從我臉上收穫鐵
一張飽含時代鐵青的臉
不可能缺鐵
鐵青深處有一雙冷峻眼睛
用沸騰的寂靜
注視著你

The Season for Harvesting Iron

Winter is the season for iron.
In the gale, all kinds of iron-sound
mixes with shattered ice, endlessly.

Iron filings shed by sorrow,
the fragments that fly off
when loneliness is hammered,
the rust of old wounds—
fall to the ground, sprout, grow.

Some bear larger hammers.
Some, astonishingly, grow feathers.
Some lengthen into blood-blurred blades.
Some bloom into sharp needles,
softly plugging the holes in the sky.

And in fact, you can harvest iron
from my face as well—
a face darkened by the iron-blue
of an era, cannot lack iron.
Deep in that iron-blue
is a pair of cold eyes
that watch you with boiling silence.

古老的清晨

樹葉將黃金
還給大地，霧散時
同學少年，站在十步外
長乳牙的古老光線
咬住冰凌墜落的弧度

一生，果真是
樹洞裡的幾粒回音？
初識的笑容，一言不合的背影
如蚊蟲落入蛛網，一晃一晃
有人甚至從未活過剎那
世界空蕩
只有手機在相愛

你我，在冬天門口
相遇，是第二次誕生
古老的清晨
翻開一本嶄新日曆

Ancient Morning

Leaves return their gold
to the earth. When the mist lifts,
an old learner—still a boy—
stands ten steps away.
Ancient light, growing its milk teeth,
bites the arc of a falling icicle.

Is a lifetime just
a few echoes in a tree hollow?
A first smile, a turned-away back
after one wrong word—
like insects caught in a web, trembling.
Some people never live
even for a moment.
The world is empty;
only cell phones are in love.

You and I, meet
at winter's doorway,
—a second birth.
An ancient morning
Opens a brand-new calendar.

舊歲

寒雨數著窗格
朝聖者迷失了偶像

粗糙的樹皮吞吐
細釉的黑光
水珠，正搬運草葉的
黑暗

饗餮散了，空椅
開始交談，繞過
孤島般空桌

我推門而出—
眾樹喧嘩。舉頭
遠方，有你

雨聲動人，飄在臉
低頭，落葉繞膝
終有一死，在漩渦中
載歌載舞—
我，頷首走過

The Old Year

Cold rain counts the windowpanes;
pilgrims lose their idols.

Rough bark inhales and exhales
a fine-glazed black light.
Water beads carry the darkness
of grass blades.

The gluttonous beast disperses;
empty chairs begin to talk,
circling island-like empty tables.

I open the door—trees erupt in clamor.
I lift my head:
there you are, in the distance.

The rain's voice moves me,
drifting across my face.
I look down—fallen leaves around my knees.
All must die in the whirlpool
they sing and dance.
I nod and walk on.

新年

聲音在黑暗中
紡出白棉花

太陽低翔
我們彎腰說話

新年一點也不新
也一點不舊
只是準時撕薄了日曆

我們還和去年一樣
說著迴圈的廢話，笑得
像一條乾淨的舊絨毯

New Year

In the dark, voices spin
white cotton.

The sun flies low;
we bend to speak.

The new year
is not new at all,
nor old—it only tears
the page from the calendar
on time.

We are still
the same as last year,
looping our nonsense, laughing
like a clean, old rug.

夢醒之間

我的笑容
在你熟睡的臉上
我未完的語詞
在你微闔的唇間

睡吧，我來照顧
這醒著的雪
這空中的冥王星

故鄉在下雨
臘梅滴落

每一滴，落在
夢醒之間的空白裡

滿地
我懸崖般的句子

Between Dream and Waking

My smile
rests on your sleeping face.
My unfinished words
lie against your barely parted lips.

Sleep—let me tend
this waking snow,
this Pluto hanging in the sky.

In my hometown
it is raining;
wintersweet drips.

Each drop
falls into the blank
between dream
and waking.

Across the ground,
my cliff-edge sentences
lie scattered.

轉化

木柴成了灰燼
它的火焰
留在你沐浴後的臉上

Transmutation

Firewood turns
to ash—
its flame
remains
on your face
after the bath.

讚美詩

感謝這乏味瑣碎的又一日
為我帶來豐沛的好奇

感謝這梳理潮濕翅膀的鳥
彷彿不再有悲傷

感謝黑，餵養
體內會發光的寂靜

感謝時間飄零之後
一座鐘樓，發出新芽

感謝這道世界的縫隙
我可以用回聲讚美

感謝雪剛下過
你帶來故鄉梅花的消息

感謝這神不守舍的晨昏
含著一個悲憫的笑

Hymn of Praise

Gratitude—
for another dull, trivial day that brings me
its abundance of curiosity;

for the bird combing its damp wings,
as if sorrow no longer existed;

for the dark, feeding the quiet
that glows inside the body;

for that after time has scattered,
a clock tower sprouts new buds;

for the seam in the world
through which my echo reaches the divine;

for snow just fallen, you bring the scent
of wintersweet from homeland;

for this absent-minded
dawn and dusk, holding
a small mercy.

數碼化

這時代，似乎一切
都能數碼化而共用，比如
你天空亂飛的鉛雲
我處驀然鳴響的汽笛
兩端的呼吸聲
這個欲雪未雪的中午

只是，這中間
山依然是連綿不斷的山
水是無數條河中奔流的水
這掌中緊握孤獨無援的溫暖
何時能數碼化

Digitization

In this era, almost everything
can be digitized and shared—
the lead-colored clouds
scattering across your sky,
the sudden train whistle where I am,
the breath at both ends,
this noon on the verge of snow.

Only—between us,
mountains are still
mountains without end;
water is still water rushing
through countless rivers.
And this warmth
held tight in my palm,
lonely, unrescued—
when can it be digitized?

秋天的眼睛

不同的眼睛，各自的風景
你我的口，說出各異的事物

岩洞口的宇宙圖景
太粉、太亮、太暗、太冷
過窄的寬，欲彰彌蓋的直言
只是偶爾，眼中刀鋒一閃

又一個秋天, 卻沒有一根雨絲
葬禮與婚禮如常
石頭張大嘴說不出什麼
一束向日葵睜大眼睛
從未見面的老朋友

你含笑，萬物與你如此親近
我好奇，此刻
若進入你的眼眸
我能看見什麼

Autumn's Eyes

Different eyes open different worlds.
Our mouths release creatures
that do not recognize each other.

At the cave's lip, the universe flickers—
too pink, too blinding, too chilly,
wide is too narrow, a cover-up
that sounds like calling a spade a spade
Occasionally one can see
a flash of the steel sharpness

Another autumn arrives
without a single strand of rain.
Funerals and weddings still go on.
Stones gape, speechless.
A sunflower stares back—
an old friend from a life never lived.

You smile, and the world
leans to bond with you
I wonder—if I stepped
into your pupils right now,
what world would open its door?

請原諒荒涼的麥田

夜晚的邊緣
另一邊，這一邊
舌頭因憂傷而醒來
又含著歡樂打盹

耳語的肌膚
冰涼又溫暖
秋雨嘀滴嗒嗒
在金黃稻草酣睡裡

像鳥兒原諒初冬無頭的麥田
寬恕這醒來又困乏的語辭
對內心深藏的愛無能為力吧
事物美好在於它的局限

Forgive the Desolate Wheatfield

At the edge of night—
the other side, and this side—
the tongue wakes from sorrow,
then dozes again
with joy in its mouth.

Skin that whispers,
cold and warm at once.
Autumn rain ticks softly
inside the golden
sleep of straw.

Like a bird forgiving
the headless wheatfield of early winter,
forgive these words
that wake only to grow weary again.
We are helpless before the love
buried deepest within.
Things are beautiful
because they are limited.

秋天的聲音

琥珀吉他上，藍色的手
秋風正翻找一首老歌的地址
水龍頭滴落清冽的全音階
潔白瓷盤奏出佳餚的七和絃
正楷的笑聲，草寫的安靜

靠著未修好的門框，我看見
生活蟲洞，湧出喧嘩
暮色中，落葉的手指晃動
想抓住什麼，在空中
發出近乎愉悅的悲傷切分音

被聲音遺忘，被聲音緊握

有聲的事物都是荒謬的
而無聲的事物更加錯誤
若不曾與你同涉塵世的交響
若你不在那寂靜的軸心

The Sound of Autumn

On an amber guitar, a blue hand.
The autumn wind rummages for an old song.
The faucet drips a clear full scale,
white porcelain plates play seventh chords
of fine food, laughter in block script,
and quiet in cursive.

Leaning against an unrepaired doorframe,
I see a wormhole in daily life spilling noise.
In the dusk, the fingers of fallen leaves
tremble—trying to grasp something,
striking the air with syncopation
of almost-joyful sorrow.

Forgotten by sound, held tight by sound.

All things that make noise are absurd;
all things without noise are even more mistaken—
unless I had walked with you
through the world's symphony,
unless you stood
at the stillness of its axis.

致未識的傾聽者

殘缺是一種仁慈

堅岩的裂縫
窄門，讓陽光
可以聽見黑暗湧出之聲

深信你的真實存在
一塊鐵
就突然有了軟肋

起風了
蘆葦波湧，幾乎折斷
傾聽的完美弧度

空缺陶器，接住
未抵達的聲響

聽見，汽笛苦行的腳步
踏著鏽跡的鐵軌而來

To the Listener Not Yet Met

Brokenness is a kind of mercy.

A fissure in solid rock—
a narrow gate through which sunlight
can hear the darkness surge.

Believing in the truth
of your existence,
a piece of iron suddenly
grows a soft spot.

The wind rises, reeds swell
and nearly snap—
the perfect curve of listening.

An empty vessel catches
a sound that has not yet arrived.

I hear the footsteps
of a pilgrim-train whistle
coming along rust-scarred rails.

及時向溺水的魚援手

好孩子，眼裡總有活兒
不用提醒就及時去做

看見黑，趕緊潑一桶墨汁
黑得更濃，好讓閃電現身

就像那條藍色的裙
主動把海風引到正確方向

就像堅硬的漂木
及時向溺水的魚伸出援手

就像這十一月早晨
為我們準備了溫暖的蕭瑟

Lending Hands to Drowning Fish

A good kid's eyes can always see
what to do—no need to remind in time.

Seeing darkness, then hurry to throw
a bucket of black ink to it
so lightning can reveal itself.

Like that blue dress that takes initiatives
to guide the sea wind to a proper direction.

Like a piece of hardened driftwood
reaching out
to save a drowning fish.

Like this November morning
preparing for us
a warmth made of desolation.

肉身是不断流逝的时光

夜來到破曉這一刻
從鬃到尾，黑咕隆咚
黑色的風搖撼黑色的樹

長翅膀的耳朵，送來
你發光的身體
臥在我漆黑的懷中
貓也在旁，閉著眼，粉紅的爪
把兩個世界踩成一個琥珀的窩
均勻的鼾聲，零碎夢囈、嗯哦
舉證你，在別處宜家宜室
表明我，在他方養家糊口

冷風中溫暖的存在
火車的汽笛，由遠及近
隱約的車輪轟隆聲
肉身是不停流逝的時光

The Body Is Time Disappearing

Night arrives at the instant
before dawn, a dense blackness
from mane to tail. Black wind
shakes black trees.

Winged ears carry to me
your luminous body,
lying in the darkness
of my arms. The cat beside us,
eyes closed, pink paws pressing two worlds
into a single amber nest.
Even breathing, broken murmurs,
soft oh-sounds—all testifying
that you belong to a home elsewhere,
and I to a livelihood
in another place.

A warm presence in the cold wind.
A train whistle, approaching from far away.
The faint rumble of wheels.
The body is time
ceaselessly passing.

浮士德之花

蕾絲邊的手，漂浮在黑暗中
捧起明豔花朵——易碎的契約
無情的鐘錶，偶爾生出柔腸

別用下一秒花的凋零
來阻止這一秒的盛開
別用下一秒的雨
遮蔽這一秒的陽光——

愛的屋頂，千瘡百孔
別作聲，且任光、雨傾瀉
也別跑出這幢房屋
外面會更冷

面具戴畢，劇場開演：
希臘悲劇、中世紀神秘劇
巴羅克寓言劇、百老匯歌舞劇
獨白、暗示、旋轉，呼天搶地
但你也可在臺上呼呼大睡

菱形秋水上，那只船
漂來蕩去，來回擺渡——

Faust's Flower

A lace-edged hand floats in the dark,
lifting a vivid blossom—a fragile contract.
The pitiless clock
occasionally grows a tender gut.

Do not use the flower's next-second wilting
to stop this second's bloom.
Do not let the next-second rain
cover this second's sun.

The roof of love is full of wounds.
Make no sound—let light and rain
pour through. And do not flee
this house; it is colder outside.

Masks on, the theater begins:
Greek tragedy, medieval mystery play,
Baroque allegory, Broadway musical—
monologues, hints, spins, wailing.
You may also fall fast asleep onstage.

On the diamond-shaped autumn water,
a boat drifts, ferrying back and forth—

天曉得有什麼發生
經歷便是命運——
我經歷，故我在

讓愛情繼續痛恨詩人
他們長歎短籲，粉飾傷口
哲學家更有害——
花掉這一秒去憂思下一秒

也須遠離道德飽學之士
一本殘缺的幾何倫理讀本
規定了愛情的合理形狀
但愛情偏偏是漩渦、裂縫
不規則多邊形、變形

喊出這暴烈的美，要喊出來：
時光啊，你如此絕倫——
請在此刻停駐！
但沒有什麼可以停下
時間，只是一個逃避的藉口

God knows what is happening.
Experience is destiny—
I experience, therefore I am.

Let love continue to despise poets—
their sighs, their patched-over wounds.
Philosophers are worse—spending this second
to worry about the next.

And keep away from moral scholars
whose incomplete geometry of ethics
dictates the proper shape of love.
But love is a whirlpool, a fissure,
an irregular polygon, a deformation.

Shout this violent beauty—shout it out:
Time, you are incomparable—
stay here, in this moment!
But nothing can stay.
Time is only an excuse
for escape.

二人拾柴

說著說著
雪就下了起來

雪，赤裸雙足
行走於火焰之中

我們一直說著
不斷朝火中添些乾柴

We Are Gathering Firewood

Talking,
and talking—
snow begins to fall.

Snow,
bare-footed,
walking through fire.

We keep talking,
and keep feeding dry wood
into the flames.

他的故事

晃蕩一生的老男人
回到故鄉——廢棄的鋼鐵之都
聽見少年的自己走在雪地上
眼睛吹著口哨
站在自己的時空之外
讀著自己在時間裡的故事

匹茲堡午夜的機器聲
跳舞的但丁
被遺忘的巴黎小旅館
窗外，德彪西灑下月光羽毛
托斯卡納的田野，飛翔的耳朵
愛琴海閃耀的水波跌宕
遍佈石頭的灼熱曠野
走過愛人的暗影

空闊林中，葉落盡
他高聲地歌唱
那些曾經的愛人
深藏在內心最隱秘的抽屜裡
她們心臟在他右眼的瞳孔中跳動
那些，柔嫩的唇

His Story

An old man drifted all his life
returns to his hometown—
the abandoned capital of steel.
He hears his younger self walking across the snow,
eyes whistling, standing outside
his own slice of spacetime,
reading the story he once lived inside.

Midnight machines in Pittsburgh.
Dante dancing.
A forgotten little hotel in Paris.
Outside, Debussy scatters feathers of moonlight.
Tuscan fields, ears taking flight.
The Aegean, its glittering waves
rising and falling. A burning wilderness
strewn with stones. The shadow of a lover
he once walked through.

In a wide forest stripped of leaves,
he sings aloud for all the lovers
he once had are hidden in the innermost drawer
of his heart. Their hearts beat inside the pupil
of his right eye—
those tender lips.

他把過往生活撕碎
然後，在秋風中
又把這些碎片一一拼接
就像拼回複雜的拼圖
理解了幸福的各個零件——
半根羽毛、一滴酒、殘句
通曉了悲傷的構成——
匍匐在地找到的一根頭髮
為了忘記所有的愛人
他把她們寫成詩

隔著七座山，七條河
暗夜的十指緊扣
濕潤的火苗四目相投
聽著那二十只鐘
影子的唇、磨損的機器
在林中奏響，此起彼伏——
彷佛那也是我們的一生

He tears his past life into pieces,
then in the autumn wind
fits them back together, like reassembling
a complicated puzzle.
He understands the components of happiness—
half a feather, a drop of wine, a broken line.
He grasps the structure of sorrow—
a single hair
found crawling on the ground.
To forget all his lovers,
he writes them into poems.

Across seven mountains and seven rivers,
ten fingers interlace in the dark.
Moist flames meet each other's gaze.
Twenty clocks ring in the distance—
the lips of shadows, the worn-down machines
echoing through the forest,
rising and falling—
as if that, too, were our life.

電流上， 小紙船

載浮載沉，將去往何方

On the current, a tiny paper boat

rises and sinks—where will it go

她和他

一、
夕陽把窗簾吹飛起來
水光流轉的梨
懷抱一片欲墜的枯葉
透明的暗影晃動

對望的山巒褪下胭脂
溫暖的脊背比河岸更荒蕪
小母馬鬃毛的火焰
在水面上無助地燃燒

世界這般遼闊
窗戶這麼小
愛的刻痕，冰涼又燙手
你會在哪個方向出現

二、
晨曦的指尖撥響鬧鐘
廢墟庭院的公雞
雄渾的啼鳴，沒排上用場
依然深陷於
一場工作事故的夢

She and He

I.
The sunset blows the curtain into the air.
A pear, shimmering with water-light,
cradles a leaf about to fall.
A transparent shadow trembles.

The facing mountains shed their rouge.
A warm back more desolate than a riverbank.
The flame of a young mare's mane
burns helplessly on the surface of water.

The world is this vast;
the window this small.
Love's carved marks—cold yet burning.
From which direction will you appear.

II.
Dawn's fingertips pluck the alarm clock.
The rooster in the ruined courtyard—
its mighty crow never used—
still trapped in a dream
of a workplace accident.

針尖上，黑虎
踏著亮晶晶的鏽蹄
黑須間露出潔白的虎牙
坍塌的牆上，輝煌的夢遺
猶如殘缺的王國地圖

寬敞的街，狹窄手機的臉
孤獨得像聳動的人群
你出現，打開閘門
電弧四溢，湧出一條緞帶般焊縫
幸福液體泛著憂傷漣漪
電流上， 小紙船
載浮載沉，將去往何方

On the needle's tip, a black tiger
steps with hooves shining with rust.
Between its whiskers, white fangs gleam.
On the collapsed wall,
a glorious nocturnal emission—
like a broken map of a kingdom.

A wide street, the narrow face of a phone—
lonely as a heaving crowd.
You appear, opening the gate.
Arcs of electricity burst outward,
a ribbon-like weld seam surging forth.
A liquid happiness ripples with sorrow.
On the current, a tiny paper boat
rises and sinks—where it will go?

拼音的混淆

知道了這個世界有你
就像發明了棉花糖
於是，那些個已黯爐的字
開始熠熠生輝
火推遲了把自己交給水
石頭奔馳在海面上
黑鳥在前引路
追逐駿馬以盜取它噴出的鼻息
興奮地在鍵盤上敲擊
打著拼音："愛上"
電腦給出"哀傷"二字
為此，黑鳥用你的嘴唇
朝我的耳朵會心一笑

The Confusion of Pinyin

Knowing that you exist in this world
is like inventing cotton candy.
Those words long reduced to ash
begin to glow again.
Fire delays its surrender to water.
Stones racing across the sea,
a black bird leads the way,
chases a stallion to steal the breath
bursting from its nostrils.
Excited, I tap at the keyboard,
typing the pinyin for
“fall in love.”
The computer returns
the characters for “sorrow.**”
For this, the black bird
borrows your lips
and gives my ear
a knowing smile.

** Pinyin for Chinese “fall in love” and “sorrow” sound similar.

一种病

秋霜點燃了半壁江山
紅火焰，黑火焰，白火焰，紫火焰
在枝頭，她們高高低低
用火苗，輪番擦拭天空的虛無

喜劇家阿裡斯多芬打完了嗝
放下酒杯，口吐真言
愛神最偉大之處
在於給人類治好了一種病

劈開的殘缺，所以愛
不再擁有，所以愛
惟有它，導向缺失的另一半
取回最初的完滿

可是，你還是改了吧
就像種菊，得掐去多餘花苞
怎麼辦，容我再想會
每一朵風姿卓絕，各有各的好

上古神俄刻阿諾斯和海之女神泰西絲
生下三千女兒，塞王海妖和繆斯

A Kind of Illness

Autumn frost sets half the land ablaze—
flames, red, black, white, violet,
on the branches, rise and fall.
Their fire-tips taking turns
to polish the sky's emptiness.

Aristophanes the comedian
finishes his hiccup, sets down his cup,
and speaks the truth:
Eros heals the wound
that split the first beings in two.

Incompleteness—therefore love,
no longer possessing—therefore love.
Only love leads us toward the missing other half,
restoring the original wholeness.

But still, please restrain yourself—
to grow chrysanthemums, pinch off extra buds is must.
What now, let me think again.
Each blossom so exquisite with its own grace.

Okeanos of old and Tethys, goddess of the sea,
bore three thousand daughters— Sirens and Muses,

逐水而生，青春不老，卻會死亡
每一位都可能是我另一半自己

那另一半自己，流落何方
誰是真愛人，美少年
就連睿智的蘇格拉底
也無法確認阿爾西比亞德斯眼神

真的不能保證這位就是
或許只是一個贗品
這是病，得治
治病，得有真藥、真福氣

必須通過愛她們每一個
才能找到你
如同必須走完天下的歧途
我才能抵達你

born of water, forever young, yet mortal.
Any one of them could be my other half.

Where has that other half wandered?
Who is the true beloved, the handsome youth?
Even wise Socrates could not decipher
the gaze of Alcibiades.

Truly no guarantee this one
is the one—perhaps only a counterfeit.
This is an illness, and it must be treated.
To cure it
requires real medicine, real fortune.

I must love every one of them
in order to find you—
just as I must walk every wrong road
in the world
before I can arrive at you.

星辰時刻

悲傷有溫暖的面孔
就像一隻空了的蜜罐

香噴噴的杏仁，回憶
那潔白結實的牙，咬著

柿子樹，甜美小紅燈籠晃動
在失智媽媽的養老院中

桂花大叔的照相機，清脆快門聲
拍下那些來不及愛的女人

悲傷是一種未遂的快樂
悲傷是一種已遂的快樂

一起傾聽星辰的回聲吧
同事領養的新狗可還膽卻

The Hour of Stars

Sadness has a warm face—
like a honey jar emptied out.

Fragrant almonds, a memory
of those white, strong teeth biting down.

On the persimmon tree, sweet red lanterns
sway in the nursing home
where your mother loses her way.

Uncle Osmanthus and his camera—
the crisp shutter capturing women
He never had time to love.

Sadness is a joy that never happened.
Sadness is a joy that already has.

Come—let us listen to the echo
of the stars. Is the new dog
your colleague adopted still afraid of
strangers?

還缺什麼

我已備好相遇的場景
用十斤烈酒，雇魯智深倒拔
那棵纏人的柳
在那一彎新月上鑽了小孔
穿上紅線，讓它漂浮成
過去節日走失那枚的氣球
手機錄上人海茫茫的聲音
用以甄別你安靜的弧線

翻開萬年曆，仔細斟酌
選好一個曾經
錯過的著名良辰
避開驟雨初歇，曉風殘月
現在，我努力加餐飯
盼自己，早日長回到過去
成為你夢中，一直
心無旁騖呼喚的
那位，完整的成熟

What Else Is Still Missing

I have prepared the scene of our encounter.
With bottles of hard liquor, I hire Lu Zhishen
to uproot that noisy willow.
On the crescent, I drill a small hole,
thread it with red string,
let it float as the long-lost balloon
from some past festival.
On my phone, I record the roar
of vast human voices, so I can recognize
the quiet curve that is you.

I open the perpetual calendar,
carefully selecting a famous moment
that we once missed.
I avoid "rain newly ceased,"
"dawn wind, waning moon."
Now, I work hard to eat more,
hoping I can grow back
into the past—become the one
your dreams have always called for
with undivided heart:
that complete, mature person.

理想國

倉庫堆滿星球的廢品
過期的軌道，空油箱的理想
一個巨大球體上
複製了此岸與彼岸所有美景
鋪陳理想國的最佳場地

大同世界的正確配方，是什麼
托勒密地心說加多少普世價值冰塊
哥白尼日心論兌幾升烏托邦蒸餾水
白骨喧嘩，一群術士莫衷一是

也曾筆湧江山氣
花費了五十公斤的夢
氣喘吁吁，醒來
撫摸狼的臉
花白鬍鬚像飄揚旗幟

那只蕾絲邊的手
仍在漆黑的空中漂浮
持著半截燭光
呀呼，我看見了什麼

Utopia

A warehouse piled with the scrap of planets—
expired orbits, ideals with empty fuel tanks.
On a massive sphere I copy every beauty
of this shore and the other,
laying out the perfect ground for Utopia

What is the correct recipe for Great Unity,
how many cubes of universal values
to add to Ptolemy's earth-centered theory?
How many liters of utopian distilled water
to mix into Copernicus' sun-centered one?
Bones clatter, a circle of magicians cannot agree.

Once, my brush surged
with the breath of mountains and rivers.
I spent fifty kilograms of dreams.
Panting, I woke and stroked
the face of a wolf—its graying beard
fluttering like a flag.

That lace-edged hand still floats
in the pitch-dark air,
holding half a candle's light.
Yahoo—what is that I see.

啊，你自己，我自己
惟有合在一起
才會出現的我自己、你自己
理想國的淨土，成為自己的我們

你的半壁江山半個朱紅的窗
我的半壁江山半個朱紅的窗
完整的世界，逝去的一切還在
啊，好美，請停一停

Ah—yourself, myself.
Only together do we become
the you-that-is-me, the me-that-is-you.
The pure land of the ideal realm:
the "us" that becomes itself.

Your half of the world—
half a vermilion window.
My half of the world—
half a vermilion window.
A complete world,
where everything lost still remains.
Ah—how beautiful.
Let it pause for a moment.

火車這時總會來

那些寧靜的中午
秋天的天空高得沒有著落
有時雲特別亂

靠在世界的兩端
精煉地，絮絮叨叨
既日常又不著邊際

火車這時總會來
沿著鏽跡斑斑的鐵軌
越過枕木與枕木的間隙
鳴響長長的汽笛

它在我們之間來回奔跑
似乎在傳遞
一些難以言說的東西

每當此時，我們發怔
閉上眼睛，讓汽笛馳過
亂雲般的靜默

Train Always Comes at This Hour

Those quiet noons—
autumn sky rising so high, nowhere to rest
and messy clouds scattering sometimes.

Leaning at the two ends of the world,
we speak in a refined yet rambling way—
ordinary, but drifting beyond the edges.

The train always comes at the instant,
running along rust-scarred rails,
crossing the gaps between sleepers
blowing its long whistle.

It runs back and forth between us,
as if carrying something
that cannot be spoken.

Each time, we fall still,
close our eyes, and let the whistle
rush through—a silence
as tangled as the clouds.

攀升的夏夜

拿出各自的一半
結合成那把完整的鑰匙
我們，打開同一個夜晚
將彼此世界的碎片
拼出一輪圓月

風拂肌膚，有如嘉語
星斗在室內滑翔
韶華的暗影，也在打轉
有的就停歇在肩膀上
聽我們說話
一起聽流水般四溢的無聲
不著一字，自生雙翼

那些夏夜真短暫啊
僅僅比永恆，多出一寸呼吸

The Ascending Summer Night

We take out our separate halves
and fit them together into a single key.
With it, we open the same night
and piece together a full moon
from the fragments of our two worlds.

The wind brushes skin like kind words.
Stars glide through the room.
The shadow of youth circling there
some of it settling on our shoulder,
minding to us speak,
and listening with us to the flowing,
overflowing silence that grows wings
without a single word.

How brief those summer nights were—
only one breath, longer than eternity.

在各自小路，一起散步

雨剛下過，樹葉仍滴滴答答
六月豐盛雨水
像一場誤植的春天
腐朽的事物重新茁壯成長
並結出眼睛與耳朵的青果

隔著一大片雨雲
我們交談，進入林中小道
盛開的忍冬，散發
去年的香氣
迫不及待地伸出
金色的左手和銀色的右手
教我們，如何用舊信箋
折疊成一隻紙鳥
飛回到從前

槐花也懂得這些事
但被雨水打落得滿地都是
芬芳的殘骸
比完整時更令人恍惚
你說你記得這些童年的芬芳

Walking Together in Separate Paths

Rain just passed, the leaves still drip
June's abundant water
feels like a misplaced spring—
rotting things grow strong again
and bear green fruit of eyes and ears.

Across a wide sheet of rain-cloud,
we talk as enter the forest path.
The honeysuckle in bloom
releases last year's fragrance,
eagerly extending its golden left hand
and silver right, teaching us
how to fold an old letter into a paper bird
that flies back to before.

The locust blossoms know these things too,
but rain has beaten them to the ground—
fragrant remains
more bewildering than when whole.
You say you remember this childhood scent,

在鼻尖跳躍，癢癢的感覺

天幾乎黑了下來
我們還在交換彼此的眼前風景
一隻鹿跑過，一秒鐘的影子
希臘式露天小劇場亮起橘黃的燈
一群人戴著口罩
隨著鋼琴哼鳴，藤蔓冒出籬笆
準備瘟疫後第一場歌舞劇

jumping at the tip of your nose,
a tickling feeling.

The sky is almost dark now, yet we keep
 exchanging the scenery before our eyes.
A deer runs past—a one-second shadow.
The Greek-style amphitheater lights its amber lamps.
A masked crowd hums with the piano;
vines push through the fence,
preparing the first musical
after the plague.

舊木頭

我有一根舊木頭

它可能是火焰尋找的家鄉
也可能是一隻船的故居

船仍在海上遊蕩
火焰在天空撒下灰燼

這根舊木頭悲憫地笑著
但火焰和船，沒看到它的嘴唇

Old Timber

I have a piece of old wood.

It might be the homeland
fire has been searching for,
or the former dwelling of a boat.

The boat still wanders the sea.
The fire scatters ash across the sky.

The old timber
smiles with pity—
but neither the fire
nor does the boat see its lips.

節令：大雪

我在棉花内部遇见你
这是十二月
黑鸟在外面大声告警
碎冰的箭矢横飞
到处是冻伤
正沿着电话线蔓延
滋滋作响

烛焰舔舐夜的边缘
我们用棉花的纤维交谈
困了，就打个盹
贝壳半开
温暖的声线
穿过肝肠寸断的欢乐
还原为新生的婴语

纠缠如乱发
却不纠缠什么

Solar Term: Major Snow

I meet you inside the cotton.
It is December.
A black bird outside alarm us loudly.
Shards of ice fly like arrows.
Frostbite spreads along
the telephone wires,
crackling.

Candle flame licks the edge of night.
We speak through the fibers
of the cotton. When tired, we doze—
a shell half-open,
a warm voice
passing through devastated joy,
returning
to newborn babble.

Tangled like loose hair,
yet tangled
with nothing.

語詞不太需要有意義

一對小鳥睡眼惺忪
溫暖的舌頭，打著結

羽毛已靠在一起
語詞不太需要有意義

就像星星重複星星
陽光抄襲著陽光

誰也沒在意
沒日沒夜地語義迴圈

Words Don't Really Need Meaning

Two small birds, drowsy,
their warm tongues tied in a knot.

Words don't really need meaning.
Since their feathers
leaning together already.

Just as stars repeat stars,
sunlight copies sunlight.

No one notices
the endless, day-and-night
loop of meaning.

最近的遠，不來之來

如愛人合體，燭光滴落

The nearest far, the arrival that never arrives—

like lovers joining into one, candlelight drips.

燭光滴落

汽笛奔來又離去
教堂的鐘，咳嗽著
時間真的老了
沒趕上自己開的火車
霧與初雪，瓜分著白色

大地像一堆過了期的雜誌
無所事事的鳥
偶兒翻幾頁，漿果大拍賣舊廣告
紙亂飄，文字滾落一路
落日與懸鈴木共用著影子

生銹的冰涼鑿子
用思想中的一縷芳香
雕琢出溫暖的頸窩
最近的遠，不來之來
如愛人合體，燭光滴落

Dripping Candlelight

The whistle rushes in and out.
The church bell coughs—
time has truly grown old, missing the train
that it set for itself. Fog and first snow
divide the color white between them.

The earth is like a stack of expired magazines.
Idle birds flip a few pages—old berry-sale ads.
Paper scatters, words roll down the road.
The sunset shares its shadow
with the plane trees.

A rusty, cold chisel
uses a single thread of imagined fragrance
to carve a warm hollow of a neck.
The nearest far, the arrival that never arrives—
like lovers joining into one,
candlelight drips.

溫暖的冬雨

溫暖的蕭瑟
鳥在不遠處發出春天的啼鳴
瘟疫的又一年接近尾聲
兩個世界
在黑白電影中
雨點綿密，敲擊天窗

這兒也在下雨
並送來歌聲，“哈利路亞”
那位穿灰色僧袍的浪子早已離世
混聲無伴奏的吟哦代替他活著
你的信仰很堅定
但需要一種切膚的證實

Warm Winter Rain

A warm desolation.
Birds nearby give out the cries
of spring. Another year
of the plague draws to its end.
Two worlds, in a black-and-white film—
rain falling dense,
tapping on the skylight.

It is raining here as well,
bringing with it a song—
"Hallelujah."
The wanderer in the gray monk's robe
has long since died;
a mixed-voice a cappella hum
lives in his place.
Your faith is steadfast, yet it asks
for a proof that cuts to the bone.

鸡毛信

木星與土星正在會面
必定是，木星上的某一位
發了一封雞毛信
給土星上的某一位

八百年了，木星還是單身
內部飽含激情的風暴
土星戴著光環
神秘纏繞著，婚否不明

拿撒說，銀河系充滿了文明
但基本上都已死去
儘管以前相互經常發雞毛信
我覺得，拿撒在妒忌

此刻，我也等著雞毛信
像木星與土星那樣
見上面，說點什麼或不作聲
都是極好的

Urgent Letter with Feathers

Jupiter and Saturn are meeting again.
Surely someone on Jupiter
has sent an urgent letter with feather
to another on Saturn.

Eight hundred years—Jupiter is still single,
yet its storms full of passion.
Saturn wears its rings,
mysterious, marital status unknown.

NASA says the galaxy is full
of civilizations, but most died already.
Though they used to
exchange feather letters
all the time—
I think NASA is jealous.

And now, I too wait for a letter,
like Jupiter and Saturn—
to meet, to say something
or say nothing.
Either way, it would be
perfect.

暴風雪正從西邊過來

電話裡，我聽見
你那邊一群烏鴉在叫
也不知道，我臉上一道新刀口
對你耳語了什麼
我說，讀了幾篇琳達·葛列格
在一堆空椅子之間寫往日
感覺她是我失散多年的密友
你居然嗯了一聲
好像我說的她，和你是同一個人
暴風雪，正從西邊過來

Blizzard Is Coming from the West

On the phone, I hear
a flock of crows calling from your side.
I don't know what the new cut
on my face
whispered into your ear.

I said I'd been reading
Linda Gregg—
writing the past among a cluster
of empty chairs. She feels
like a long-lost friend of mine.

And you—
you actually murmured
"mm," as if the "she" I spoke of
were the same person
as you.

The blizzard is coming
from the west.

在巴賽隆納高迪教堂前

神與果皮接壤的街角
我尋找那只神聖的垃圾桶——
它曾吞下你完整的笑聲
如今被過客影子的遺骸撐變形

建了上百年的教堂
一半還在建，一半開始懷舊
腳手架結出塑膠鳳梨——
像時間在模仿自然的錯誤
工匠用金粉填補聖像的皺紋
牆上的鴿子，鐵屑般
飛向靜默的鐘聲

仿佛要讓時間重新開始

吹過你亂髮的風也吹過我的亂髮
在聖像的石髮間低語
街頭歌手，撙奏吉他蛛絲
對著河流般一群群影子吟唱
"哦，多麼美妙的世界"

歌聲在空中打轉
就像它曾經在你身邊環繞

In Front of Gaudí's Cathedral

At the street corner where God meets fruit peels,
I search for that sacred trash bin—
the one that once swallowed your entire laughter,
now warped by the remains of passing shadows.

A cathedral built for over a century—
half still under construction, half grows nostalgic.
Scaffolding sprouts plastic pineapples,
as if time were imitating nature's mistakes.
Artisans fill the saints' wrinkles
with gold dust. Pigeons on the wall,
like iron filings, fly toward the silent bells.

As if trying to restart time.

The wind that tousled your hair
tousles mine as well,
whispering through the stone hair
of the statues. A street singer
plucks threads of guitar webbing,
singing to the river-like flow of shadows:
"Oh, what a wonderful world."

The song circles in the air,
just as it once circled around you.

光找到了
少年的某片彩玻璃
照亮這一瞬間
我靜靜聽著
那些滲入教堂石材裡
未曾說出的話

Light finds
a shard of stained glass
from someone's youth,
illuminating this moment.
I listen quietly
to the words that seep into the stone
of the cathedral—
words never spoken.

www.ingramcontent.com/pod-product-compliance
Lightning Source LLC
LaVergne TN
LVHW042356150826
845671LV00022B/360/J

* 9 7 9 8 9 9 4 3 4 9 9 1 5 *